IDENTIFYING AND BREAKING
CURSES

IDENTIFYING AND BREAKING
CURSES

JOHN ECKHARDT

Whitaker House

Unless otherwise indicated, all Scripture quotations are taken from the King James Version (KJV) of the Holy Bible.

IDENTIFYING AND BREAKING CURSES

Crusaders Ministries
P.O. Box 7211
Chicago, IL 60680

ISBN: 0-88368-615-5
Printed in the United States of America
Copyright © 1999 by John Eckhardt

Whitaker House
30 Hunt Valley Circle
New Kensington, PA 15068

Library of Congress Cataloging-in-Publication Data

Eckhardt, John, 1957–
  Identifying and breaking curses / by John Eckhardt.
    p. cm.
  ISBN 0-88368-615-5 (pbk. : alk. paper)
  1. Blessing and cursing. 2. Spiritual warfare. I. Title.
  BV4509.5 .E34 20000
  248—dc21   00-009172

1 2 3 4 5 6 7 8 9 10 11 12 13 / 08 07 06 05 04 03 02 01 00

Contents

Foreword

Do failure and frustration seem to be your lot in life? Is your life characterized by continual set-backs and misfortune? Does it appear as though no matter what you do in life, you cannot seem to obtain the blessings of the Lord?

Often the most frustrating thing about this whole scenario is the fact that you are a believer and love the Lord. Is it possible for a born-again, Spirit-filled believer to still be living under a curse?

If so, how can a believer be delivered from a curse and be set free to obtain and walk in the full blessing of the Lord?

Redeemed from the Curse

According to Galatians 3:13, we are redeemed from the Curse. In other words, Jesus became a curse in our stead. If this is true, then how can a believer still be under a curse?

Identifying and Breaking Curses

To understand this, we need to know the difference between what is legally ours and what is experientially ours. Just because something is legally ours does not mean we will automatically obtain it and walk in it.

What makes this even truer in spiritual matters is the fact that we have an adversary, the Devil, who is determined to keep away from us what is legally ours. If he can keep you ignorant of what is legally yours, he can still enforce a curse against you, even though you are legally redeemed from it.

The same is true in the case of sickness and disease. Although the Word of God teaches that we are already healed by the stripes of Jesus (Isaiah 53:5), there are many believers who have not appropriated this promise and continue to battle with sickness. This is because healing is a part of our redemption, but it is not automatic.

Again, according to the Word of God, we are healed by the stripes of Jesus. However, though every believer has been legally redeemed from sickness, there are still many sick believers. Just because one is a believer does not make one exempt from sickness. It is possible for a believer to be sick even with healing being a part of our redemption.

Unfortunately, there are still many believers living under curses even though they have been legally redeemed from curses. Just as a believer may have to fight a good fight of faith for healing, he or she may also have to fight a good fight of faith against curses.

So the answer to the question, "Can a believer be under a curse?" is, "Legally, no; but experientially, yes."

This is to say, Satan may not have a legal right to enforce a curse against you, but he is an outlaw and will attempt to do so anyway.

Therefore, curses oftentimes have to be broken over the lives of believers, and the believers must learn how to stand in faith against those curses, keeping them from operating in their lives.

The promises in the Word are not automatic. They must be believed and often fought for. You don't have to fight God for His promises; He is not keeping them back from you. But you must contend with the Adversary who is trying to prevent you from receiving and walking in God's promises.

So if you are a believer and you are experiencing the symptoms of a curse, you will have to be loosed from it before you will be able to walk in the full blessings of the Lord.

Chapter One

Definition of a Curse

Let us first give a biblical definition of a curse. What does the Word of God have to say about the subject of curses? A curse is God's *"recompense"* (Lamentations 3:65) in the life of a person and his or her descendants as a result of iniquity. The curse causes sorrow of heart and gives demonic spirits legal entry into a family whereby they can carry out and perpetuate their wicked devices.

There are several words we will define in order to give a clearer picture and a better understanding of how curses operate. They are as follows: *recompense; iniquity* and *perversion; persecution;* and *destruction.*

> *Render unto them a recompense, O LORD, according to the work of their hands. Give them sorrow of heart, thy curse unto them. Persecute and destroy them in anger from under the heavens of the LORD.*
> *(Lamentations 3:64–66)*

Identifying and Breaking Curses

➤**Recompense:** (n.) an equivalent or a return for something done, suffered, or given; (v.) to return in kind, requite, repay.

> *Thou showest lovingkindness unto thousands, and recompensest the iniquity of the fathers into the bosom of their children after them: the Great, the Mighty God, the LORD of hosts, is his name.* *(Jeremiah 32:18)*

> *Vengeance is mine; I will repay, saith the Lord.* *(Romans 12:19)*

The Lord recompenses iniquity into the bosom of the children in the form of curses. A recompense is a reward or a payment. Just as the Lord rewards righteousness, He also rewards sin. He rewards sin in the form of curses. *Webster's* definition of *reward* is "something that is given in return for good or evil done or received."

➤**Iniquity:** the Hebrew word translated *"iniquity"* in Jeremiah 32:18 is *avown*, meaning perversity, moral evil, fault, iniquity, mischief, sin.

Perversion: a turning away from what is good or morally right, diverting to a wrong end or purpose, misdirecting; stubbornness or obstinacy to what is right.

Perversion of any kind brings curses upon the children. God curses iniquity (perversion). There are different forms of perversion:

Definition of a Curse

❖ *Sexual perversion* includes adultery, fornication, incest, bestiality, homosexuality, lesbianism, oral sex, anal sex, orgies, molestation, and rape. A history of these sexual sins in the bloodline opens the door for Curses of Lust.

❖ *Financial perversion* includes the misuse of money, unjust gain, cheating, gambling, covetousness, not honoring God (by tithing), bribes, crooked means of obtaining money, illegal trafficking of drugs and alcohol, robbery, and embezzlement. A history of these sins in the bloodline can open the door for Curses of Poverty.

❖ *Religious perversion* includes idolatry, worshipping idols, ancestral worship, and oaths and pledges to idol gods. A history of these sins in the bloodline can open the door for the Curse of Idolatry and Multiple Curses.

❖ *Spiritual perversion* includes witchcraft, voodoo, sorcery, divination, occult involvement, and spiritism. A history of these sins in the bloodline can open the door for Multiple Curses.

❖ *Behavioral perversion* includes a perverse way, pride, rebellion, drunkenness, murder, returning evil for good, sinful attitudes and ways, ungodly conduct, mistreating others, abuse, and unrighteous behavior.

❖ *Familial perversion* includes perversion of the family order, Ahab and Jezebel spirits (see 1 Kings 16–21), men not taking leadership, dominating females, rebellious children, or any time God's order in the family is violated and neglected. This perversion opens the door for Curses upon Marriages and Families.

❖ *Perverse speech* includes spoken curses, vexes, hexes, spells, lying, blasphemy, slander, crooked speech, vows, oaths and pledges to idols, cults, false gods, enchantments, and bewitchments.

Iniquity is the cause of a curse. Now, let's look at the results of a curse.

Give them sorrow of heart.   (Lamentations 3:65)

The result of a curse is sorrow of heart, including failure, tragedy, frustration, death, destruction, family problems, marital problems, sickness, disease, mental illness, suicide, miscarriages, accidents, depression, sadness, sorrow, grief, vexation, torment, hopelessness, despair, poverty, lack, business failure, confusion, pain, besetting sins, stumbling blocks, guilt, shame, condemnation, lamentation, suffering, misery, bitter experiences, ill fortune, setbacks, travail, groaning, hard times, reverses, distress, calamity, mishaps, slumps, recession, and woe.

Persecute and destroy them in anger from under the heavens of the LORD.   (Lamentations 3:66)

➤**Persecution:** to harass in a manner designed to injure, grieve, or afflict; to pester; to run after with hostile intent; chase; put to flight; follow after; hunt; pursue.

This is the feeling of people who are laboring under a curse. Sorrow follows them wherever they go, and there is a feeling of being constantly harassed, chased, and persecuted in some area of their lives.

> *They hunt our steps....Our persecutors are swifter than the eagles of the heaven: they pursued us upon the mountains, they laid wait for us in the wilderness.* (Lamentations 4:18–19)

> *Our necks are under persecution: we labour, and have no rest.* (Lamentations 5:5)

➢**Destruction:** the action or process of destroying something. Curses open the door for the spirit of destruction (Osmodeus) to work with other spirits to destroy certain areas of an individual's life.

❖ *Destruction of the Mind* includes spirits of mental illness, schizophrenia, insanity, madness, and confusion.

❖ *Destruction of the Finances* includes spirits of poverty, lack, debt, and financial failure.

❖ *Destruction of the Body* includes spirits of sickness, infirmity, disease, and plagues.

Identifying and Breaking Curses

❖ *Destruction of the Family* includes spirits of death, accidents, rebellion, alcohol, strife, and Ahab and Jezebel.

Curses come as a result of God's divine justice recompensing the iniquity (perversion) of the fathers into the bosom of the children, causing sorrow of heart and opening the door for evil spirits, giving them the legal right to persecute and destroy by carrying out and perpetuating their evil devices in the lives of people under curses. Iniquity (perversion) brings curses. In whatever area the perversion occurs, a curse can come upon the descendants in that particular area. Some sins carry multiple curses.

Multiple Curses

And first I will recompense their iniquity and their sin double; because they have defiled my land, they have filled mine inheritance with the carcases of their detestable and abominable things. (Jeremiah 16:18)

Some sins are recompensed by God with multiple curses. Some sins are abominable and worthy of death. God's recompense upon these sins is greater. This we refer to as the Law of Recompense.

Although God punishes all sin, some sins receive a heavier punishment (multiple curses). An example would be witchcraft, which in the Old Testament carried with it the penalty of death: *"Thou shalt not suffer a witch to live"* (Exodus 22:18). Because this sin is so detestable, God will recompense it with greater (multiple) curses.

The result can be curses of witchcraft, death and destruction, insanity, poverty, sickness, and others. Multiple curses can also come as a result of idolatry (Leviticus 20:1–5); consulting familiar spirits, wizards, and witches (Leviticus 20:6); adultery (Leviticus 20:10); incest (Leviticus 20:11–12); homosexuality (Leviticus 20:13); and bestiality (Leviticus 20:15). All of these sins carried the death penalty in the Old Testament.

The result of all sin is death and destruction. Curses will eventually result in death and destruction. A curse is like a shadow that follows a person; it is a dark cloud that covers an individual, family, or nation of people. If this cloud is not lifted, it will destroy those under its power. Jesus came, died, and rose again to provide redemption from all curses. He does not desire for us to be ignorant of spiritual things. A knowledge of curses, how to identify them and break them, is an indispensable tool in the believer's arsenal to destroy the works of the Devil.

Chapter Two

Identifying Curses

A s has already been stated, the cause of curses is iniquity (perversion). Discernment and detection are the two primary ways to determine the type of curse a person may be under. Supernatural discernment through the Holy Spirit, including discerning of spirits and word of knowledge, has proven invaluable in difficult cases. (See 1 Corinthians 12:8, 10.)

The gift of discerning of spirits will help deliverance workers discern what spirit is operating in a person's life, and the gift of the word of knowledge can reveal the name of the curse and how far back it needs to be broken. Detection is simply seeing the problems and knowing something of the family history of the person for whom you are praying.

Some people have a limited knowledge of what sins may have been practiced by their ancestors. Of course, no one knows everything that has taken place in his or her family history, for our knowledge is limited at best, and God judges secret sins. The manifestation of the Spirit is needed in many of these cases.

Having a knowledge of curses and breaking them with a general prayer is good for everyone seeking deliverance. Since our knowledge of curses is limited, we must trust the Holy Spirit to give us the name of a specific curse, if necessary. Sometimes the Holy Spirit will pressure demons to tell a deliverance worker the name of the curse they are operating through.

Some curses need to be identified and broken by name because some demons will attempt to use those unidentified curses as a legal right to stay. Some demons are very stubborn and will not give up their ground simply because the worker says, "In Jesus' name, I break all curses."

Even though these demonic spirits have no legal right to stay based on Galatians 3:13, they will still attempt to stay if the curse has not been specifically identified and broken. We need to be as thorough as possible and leave no stone unturned in the ministry of deliverance.

Curses of the Womb

Thou...recompensest the iniquity of the fathers into the bosom of their children after them. (Jeremiah 32:18)

Identifying Curses

*Behold, I was shapen in iniquity, and in sin did my
mother conceive me.*   *(Psalm 51:5)*

*The wicked are estranged from the womb: they go
astray as soon as they be born, speaking lies.*
(Psalm 58:3)

*For I knew that thou wouldest deal very treacher-
ously, and wast called a transgressor from the womb.*
(Isaiah 48:8)

Children can be born with curses because of the
iniquity of the fathers. David stated that he was conceived in iniquity. Remember that iniquity is the cause
behind curses. Children conceived in adultery, fornication, drunkenness, rejection, and rape are especially vul-
nerable to demonic attack and open to various curses.
Because of curses, demons can enter a child while in the
womb.

Curses Affect the Household

The curse of the LORD is in the house of the wicked.
(Proverbs 3:33)

Even though the Lord deals with individuals, He
also looks upon and deals with the unit (household).

*Believe on the Lord Jesus Christ, and thou shalt be
saved, and thy house.*   *(Acts 16:31)*

Identifying and Breaking Curses

The house of the wicked shall be overthrown.
(Proverbs 14:11)

The LORD will destroy the house of the proud.
(Proverbs 15:25)

Wickedness (iniquity) can affect the entire household, including the children born into that household. Certain spirits operate in certain households because of curses.

How to Diagnose a Curse

In order to effect a true remedy, you must be able to make a proper diagnosis. Without a correct diagnosis, you will not be able to get to the root problem. If the diagnosis is a curse, then the remedy is breaking the curse according to Galatians 3:13.

The word *diagnose* is defined: "to recognize by signs and symptoms; to analyze the cause or nature of." A diagnosis is the investigation or analysis of the cause or nature of a condition, situation, or problem.

When a person goes to the doctor for a physical problem, the first thing that doctor will do is run tests to diagnose the problem. The doctor will then prescribe medication based on the diagnosis. The correct diagnosis is necessary to effect a cure.

There are many believers who are dealing with curses but have not made the correct diagnosis of their problems. The Enemy is able to hide and operate in their lives because he has not been diagnosed.

Demons operate through curses and will continue to do so in the lives of believers even though they have been redeemed from the curse, if these curses remain undetected and are not dealt with.

One of the best books available today on the subject of curses is *Blessing or Curse,* by Derek Prince. He lists seven common indications of a curse:

1. Chronic financial problems

2. Chronic sickness and disease

3. Female problems

4. Being accident-prone

5. Marital problems

6. Premature deaths

7. Mental illness

I have included two more indications that we have seen in ministering deliverance:

8. Mistreatment and abuse by other people (including mental, physical, and sexual abuse, and rejection); receiving no favor and no mercy; and being a victim of cruelty and violence.

9. Wandering, vagabondism, no place to rest or live, constantly moving from house to house, city to city, job to job, relationship to relationship.

Statements such as these can be a sign of a curse at work:

- ➤ "I seem to take one step forward and two steps backward."

- ➤ "Nothing ever seems to work out for me."

- ➤ "I never can seem to get ahead."

- ➤ "I knew something bad would happen."

- ➤ "If it were not for bad luck, I wouldn't have any luck at all."

- ➤ "This always happens to me."

- ➤ "It happened to my parents, and now it is happening to me."

Let's look at the indications or symptoms of curses in depth:

Chronic Financial Problems

The first symptom is chronic financial problems, especially if there is a history of debt, bankruptcy, poverty, and lack in the family. No matter what a person does, he or she cannot seem to get ahead financially. This person is unable to keep jobs, experiences layoffs, or has an inability to find work, especially when there is no logical explanation for it.

There are many people who struggle financially because of curses. They never can seem to escape unexpected bills, accidents causing additional bills, loss of money, car breakdowns, mechanical malfunctions, losing money (purses, wallets), loss to theft, and high interest rates.

Just when they seem to get ahead financially something happens to set them back. This can be true even if a person earns a lot of money. Again, for some people there is no logical explanation as to why they should not be further ahead financially. Illogical circumstances or events occur, such as mishandling money, a history of welfare in the family, or business failures. *"The destruction of the poor is their poverty"* (Proverbs 10:15).

The spirit of destruction works through this curse to destroy a person financially. Spirits of poverty, lack, and debt operate through this curse.

Testimony of a Pastor

I recently heard the testimony of a pastor who told of having constant car problems. Even though he had a good car, something was always going wrong with it. Every time he would take his car in for repairs, the estimates were more than he could afford. This was occurring even though he was a faithful giver. He prayed and asked the Lord why he, a faithful giver, was having so many problems with his car.

The Lord revealed to him that it was a curse, and showed him that his father and grandfather had always struggled financially and had car problems. He then prayed and broke the curse. When he took his car back for repairs, the mechanics discovered a small part that was causing all the other problems that had been esti-mated to cost thousands of dollars to repair. The amaz-ing thing was that the cost to replace the small part that had broken was less than a dollar! All of this was discovered after he broke the curse.

Financial Setbacks

A setback means that progress is slowed, hindered, or delayed.

> *Ye have sown much, and bring in little; ye eat, but ye have not enough; ye drink, but ye are not filled with drink; ye clothe you, but there is none warm; and he that earneth wages earneth wages to put it into a bag with holes.*   *(Haggai 1:6)*

The Living Bible renders this verse, *"Your income disappears, as though you were putting it into pockets filled with holes!"*

Identifying Curses

For all his days are sorrows, and his travail grief;
yea, his heart taketh not rest in the night. This is also
vanity.   *(Ecclesiastes 2:23)*

Housing

Problems with housing include foreclosures; cruel and unfair landlords; fires; floods; continuous evictions; wandering; vagabondism; lights, gas, telephone shut off; house vandalized or burglarized; heating problems; plumbing problems; roofing problems; and other housing repair problems that drain your finances.

Work

Symptoms of curses related to work include job lay-offs, pink slips, company closed down, fired for wrong reasons, missing days because of sickness, accidents on the job, abuse from bosses and fellow employees, sexual harassment, going from job to job, can't keep a job, can't hold down a job, can't find a job, just missed a job, "day late and a dollar short," "wrong place at the wrong time."

The result of all this is frustration and discouragement, followed by sadness, sorrow, depression, despair, despondency, anger, and bitterness.

Chronic Sickness and Disease

The second sign of a curse is chronic sickness and disease. *Webster's Dictionary* says that *chronic* means "marked by long duration or frequent occurrence; constantly vexing, weakening, or troubling." Signs of a curse include sicknesses from childhood that persist throughout life; sicknesses and infirmities that will not respond to medication or treatment; sicknesses that won't respond to prayer; and a history of certain illnesses in the family, including high blood sugar, diabetes, cancer, sickle-cell anemia, bone disease, and blood and respiratory diseases.

The book of Deuteronomy mentions a pestilence that cleaves (Deuteronomy 28:21). A pestilence is a contagious or infectious disease, or something that is destructive or pernicious. The *New English Bible* translates, *"The Lord cause pestilence to haunt you."* To *haunt* means "to visit often or frequently; to recur constantly; to stay around or persist, to linger." A sickness that is the result of a curse lingers. You can't seem to get rid of it. It cleaves and persists. *To cleave* means "to stick to, to adhere firmly and closely to."

Female Problems

The third sign of a curse is female problems. This curse affects the area of reproductivity. Barrenness and lack of productivity are often symptoms of a curse. When the Lord blessed the man and the woman in the Garden of Eden, He said, *"Be fruitful, and multiply"* (Genesis 1:22). Fruitfulness and multiplication are always the signs of blessing. I have ministered in areas of the world where barrenness was a major problem. Many of the women who came forth for prayer were believing to conceive and bear children.

Identifying Curses

Another symptom of a curse in this area is miscarriages. Women who have had repeated miscarriages need ministry to be delivered from grief, sadness, depression, and other spirits that cause them to blame themselves. Miscarriages can be the result of idolatry in the bloodline. (See Hosea 9:13–14.)

Female problems can also include severe cramps, tormenting pain during the monthly cycle, and tumors and growths in the abdomen, womb, fallopian tubes, and ovaries. Spirits of infirmity can operate in these areas because of curses.

Accident-Prone

The fourth sign of a curse is being accident-prone. The word *prone* means "having a tendency or inclination." Just because a person has an accident, or any of the things that follow in this section, does not mean he or she is under a curse. However, if the accidents are frequent and continuous, the person may want to investigate the possibility that a curse is in operation.

Some examples of being accident prone include car accidents (someone always running into you although you are a good driver), falling down stairs, breaking a leg (especially in the same place more than once), getting poked in the eye, accidentally choking on food, being bitten by a dog, being hurt on the job, being accidentally shot, accidentally cutting oneself, accidentally drinking poison, accidentally burning oneself, walking into a door, stepping off a curb and breaking your ankle, and so on.

When a person has a history of accidents that seem unexplainable, we suspect a curse at work. I have ministered to people who have had mishap after mishap for no explainable reason. They needed to have curses broken from their lives and deliverance ministered in order to be set free from this continuing cycle.

Marital Problems

The fifth sign of a curse is marital problems.

The curse of the LORD is in the house of the wicked: but he blesseth the habitation of the just.
(Proverbs 3:33)

One of the areas hit the hardest by curses is the household. The foundation of the household is the strength of the marriage union. If the marriage is not strong, the whole family unit is affected. Family break-down and alienation can result from a curse.

Marital problems include constant arguing, fighting, and quarreling, as well as a history of divorces or separations in the family. One of the first questions I ask people who are having marital problems is whether their parents had marital problems. It is not unusual to find that a high number of people who have serious marital problems also had parents or grandparents who were divorced or involved in multiple marriages.

A history of divorce or separation in a family, or chronic arguing and fighting between mates, may be indicative of a curse and a need of deliverance from marriage-breaking spirits.

Premature Death

The sixth sign of a curse is premature death.

Be not over much wicked, neither be thou foolish: why shouldest thou die before thy time? (Ecclesiastes 7:17)

Contrary to what many people think, a person can die before his or her time. Some people believe that whenever a person dies, it is the will of the Lord. In other words, "When your time comes, there is nothing you can do about it." The Scripture tells us we can die before our time by wickedness or foolishness. Wickedness in a family can open the door for curses of death and destruction.

But the wicked shall be cut off from the earth, and the transgressors shall be rooted out of it.
(Proverbs 2:22)

The seed of the wicked shall be cut off.
(Psalm 37:28)

Identifying and Breaking Curses

Premature death in the family can include a history of suicides, deaths by drowning, car accidents, fires, floods, heart attacks, strokes, homicides, and cancer. Curses cut the life span short. Remember, *"the wages of sin is death"* (Romans 6:23).

Mental Problems

The seventh sign of a curse is mental problems—madness, insanity, confusion—especially if there is a history of this in the family. This also includes schizophrenia, and mental and nervous breakdowns.

> *The LORD shall smite thee with madness, and blindness, and astonishment of heart.*
> *(Deuteronomy 28:28)*

> *The Lord will drive thee distracted, all benighted and crazed in thy wits.*
> *(Deuteronomy 28:28, Knox Version)*

The problem of mental illness remains baffling to the psychiatric profession. They are trying to treat a spiritual problem with humanistic theories and drugs.

Schizophrenia is a major problem in our society. Schizophrenia is a demonic problem rooted in rejection and rebellion. The roots of schizophrenia are found in a curse. Children born into families where this curse operates are susceptible to a pattern of double-mindedness and mental instability.

Identifying Curses

Abuse

The eighth sign of a curse is mistreatment and abuse. This can include physical abuse; beatings; robberies; abusive marriages; always being involved in abusive relationships; sexual abuse, including rape and incest; and verbal abuse (always coming under verbal attack for no apparent reason). Mistreatment and abuse come upon not only individuals, but also entire families and even nations of people.

Vagabondism

The ninth sign of a curse is wandering (vagabondism). Psalm 109:10 states, *"Let his children be continually vagabonds, and beg: let them seek their bread also out of their desolate places."*

Vagabonds are people who move from place to place without a fixed home. These are people who wander from place to place, city to city, job to job, without ever getting on track or having a sense of direction. They never seem to find a resting place or a place to settle down. A life of poverty and begging can also result from this curse.

Break the Cycle

Another way to describe a curse, whether it is working in the area of finances, sickness, accidents, bad marriages, or another area, is the word *cycle*. There is always a cycle of bad things occurring in increments of time, whether yearly or generationally. According to *Webster's Dictionary*, a cycle is "an interval of time during which a sequence of a recurring succession of events or phenomena is completed: a course or series of events or operations that recur regularly and usually lead back to a starting point."

A person under a curse always seems to end up back at point zero. It is like a recurring nightmare that repeats itself over and over again. I refer to the result of curses as a "demonic cycle" in the life of an individual, family, or nation. Until the curse is broken, the cycle will repeat itself over and over again.

Other terms for cycle include *recurrence, frequent, regular return, periodic, haunting,* and *incessant.* The Lord desires to deliver us from any cycle of evil and to place us in a cycle of blessing.

Chapter Three

Adversity

Another way to describe a life under a curse is the word *adversity*. Adversity includes such terms as adverse circumstances, misfortune, continual struggle, difficulty, hard life, hardship, groaning, travail, bad times, ups and downs, bitter cup, bitter pill, setback, reverse, slump, recession, depression, want, need, distress, extremity, bad luck, ill luck, no luck, raw deal, rotten hand, mishap, misadventure, calamity, catastrophe, constant loser, and scapegoat.

Other descriptors include ill-fated, unlucky, unblessed, luckless, hapless, poor, wretched, miserable, undone, unhappy, doomed, under a cloud, accident prone, one's worst enemy, "from bad to worse," and "from the frying pan into the fire." (See *Roget's Theasurus*.)

Throughout the ages, people have come up with these sayings and lines that describe a curse. The best description of a curse, however, is God's own description found in His Word.

> *The LORD shall send upon thee cursing, vexation,*
> *and rebuke, in all that thou settest thine hand unto for*
> *to do.* (Deuteronomy 28:20)

The Torah states translates the above as "calamity, panic, and frustration." The *Berkeley Version* says, *"In each enterprise to which you put your hand."*

I want to emphasize the word *frustration*. This is a good, biblical description of what it feels like to be under a curse. The dictionary definition of *frustrate* is "to induce feelings of discouragement, to make ineffectual; make vain or ineffectual all efforts, however vigorous or persistent." No matter how hard one tries, his effort never pays off. The result is discouragement.

A synonym of *frustration* is *baffle*, which means "to frustrate by confusing or puzzling." In other words, a person just can't figure out why nothing seems to work for him, especially if there is no logical reason why it shouldn't. It is like a puzzle one can't figure out. Have you ever become frustrated trying to figure out a puzzle? It's like working on a Rubik's Cube. Just when you think you have it figured out, one side comes up wrong, and you have to start the whole thing all over again.

> *And thou shalt grope at noonday, as the blind gropeth*
> *in darkness, and thou shalt not prosper in thy ways:*

Adversity

*and thou shalt be only oppressed and spoiled evermore,
and no man shall save thee.   (Deuteronomy 28:29)*

To grope means "to look for something blindly or
uncertainly." A person under a curse is always looking
for success but never can find it. The *Jerusalem Bible*
translates *"And thou shalt not propser in thy ways"* as *"And
your steps will lead you nowhere."*

The Complete Bible: An American Translation puts it,
"And shalt not make a success of your life." The *New English
Bible* says, *"You will be oppressed and robbed, day in, day
out."* In other words, the Devil is able to steal all of your
blessings because of a curse.

*Moreover all these curses shall come upon thee, and
shall pursue thee, and overtake thee, till thou be
destroyed.   (Deuteronomy 28:45)*

Notice how curses operate:

1. They come upon you.

2. They pursue you.

3. They overtake you.

To come upon means "to show up." When a curse
shows up, people's first reaction is to try to get away
from it. They try to escape and flee from it. They do

everything in their power to dodge it and shake it. *To flee* means "to run away, often from danger or evil; to hurry toward a place of security."

However, the second characteristic of a curse is that it pursues you. No matter where a person turns, a curse will chase after him. *To pursue* means "to follow in order to overtake, capture, kill, or defeat." It means "to seek or haunt." There is no escape or hiding from a curse. The only remedy is to break it and be delivered from it.

The third thing a curse does is overtake. In other words, it will eventually catch up with a person and overcome him. When a person is overtaken by a curse, the curse begins to work out its intention, which is to destroy.

Under Siege

And he shall beseige thee in all thy gates, until thy high and fenced walls come down, wherein thou trustedst, throughout all thy land. (Deuteronomy 28:52)

A person under a curse is a person under siege. No matter where a person turns and hides, the Enemy comes and lays siege. The walls of a city were built for protection to keep the enemy out. The enemy would come upon a city, surround it, and lay siege to it, until the inhabitants surrendered. *To beseige* means "to surround with armed forces."

Adversity

Everything a person trusts in for protection will fall under the siege of a curse. Some people trust in money, some in education, some in friends, and so on. It makes no difference; every wall will come down under a siege.

A City without Walls

He that hath no rule over his own spirit is like a city that is broken down, and without walls.
(Proverbs 25:28)

Life under a curse can become so frustrating that a person will lose self-control. This is equivalent to a city that is broken down and without walls. A city without walls is open for invasion. The enemy is able to come in and destroy. Frustration can lead to depression, anger, rage, and discouragement.

The *Jerusalem Bible* translation of Proverbs 25:28 says, *"An open town, and without defenses: such is a man lacking self-control."* The person is left defenseless. This is what a siege will do to an individual. A curse is like an enemy surrounding you with no route of escape. No matter where you turn, failure and frustration are there. A siege is designed to break a city down over a period of time. It is a slow death.

A person under a curse may be under attack over a period of time. He may experience years of harassment from the Enemy. Yet no matter how long it takes, the end result is destruction.

> *And among these nations shalt thou find no ease, neither shall the sole of thy foot have rest: but the* LORD *shall give thee there a trembling heart, and failing of eyes, and sorrow of mind.*   *(Deuteronomy 28:65)*

No peace and no rest are the results of a curse. The *New American Bible* translates the above as, *"An anguished heart and wasted eyes and a dismayed spirit."* According to *Webster's Dictionary, anguish* means "to suffer intense pain or sorrow." Anguish is torment and agony. It means to be in dire straits. Someone in such a poisition will despair of courage, resolution, and initiative through the pressure of sudden fear or anxiety or great perplexity.

Chapter Four

Sins of the Fathers

Thou showest lovingkindness unto thousands, and
recompensest the iniquity of the fathers into the bosom
of their children after them: the Great, the Mighty God,
the Lord of hosts, is his name.
—Jeremiah 32:18

The above verse states that *"the iniquity of the fathers"* is recompensed *"into the bosom of their children."* To *recompense* means "to pay." In other words, what the parents do will affect their children. *The Living Bible* puts it, *"You are loving and kind to thousands, yet children suffer for their fathers' sins."*

This truth is also stated in Exodus 20:5:

For I the LORD thy God am a jealous God, visiting
the iniquity of the fathers upon the children unto the
third and fourth generation of them that hate me.

Identifying and Breaking Curses

The Torah says, *"Upon the third and fourth generation of those who reject me."* The prophet Hosea prophesied,

> *Because thou hast rejected knowledge, I will also reject thee, that thou shalt be no priest to me: seeing thou hast forgotten the law of thy God, I will also forget thy children.*   *(Hosea 4:6)*

There is a relationship, then, between curses and the sins of the fathers. Sin affects not only those who commit it, but also the generations to come. This shows us the terrible consequences of sin. Sin is more than an isolated act. It can reverberate for generations to come. As we saw in chapter one, the word *iniquity* in the Old Testament is the Hebrew word *avown*, meaning "perversity."

Sin is a perverting of that which is right. God's Word is right, and whenever we deviate from it, we are guilty of iniquity. *To pervert* means "to cause to turn aside or away from what is good or true or morally right."

> *So the curse causeless shall not come.*
>   *(Proverbs 26:2)*

There is always a cause for a curse. Curses cannot affect our lives for no reason. The cause of a curse is iniquity. Iniquity is perversion, deviating from what is right. God's standard of right is His Word. When we disobey His Word and deviate from it, we open the door for the curse to enter.

The curse affects not only us, but our descendants as well. The curse will continue down the bloodline until it is stopped by repentance and by appropriating by faith the redemption provided by Christ through the Cross.

The reason curses can perpetuate themselves is that descendants are usually guilty of the same sins as the fathers. When certain sins enter into a family, they open the door for certain spirits to travel from generation to generation. We tend to learn the ways of our ancestors to some degree. It can become a cycle of destruction from generation to generation.

Jesus came to stop the cycle of death and destruction! A believer can stop this cycle through repentance and breaking the curse. We can put a stop to the workings of the Enemy in our lives, no matter how many generations he has been in operation.

Curses: A Doorway for Demons

Curses open the door for evil spirits to enter and operate. Again, these evil spirits can operate in families from generation to generation, carrying out their diabolical plan to destroy. One of the keys to deliverance is understanding and breaking curses.

Identifying and Breaking Curses

Certain spirits will not come out of people until curses are broken. Curses give these demons legal entry, and the demons will use curses as a legal excuse to remain.

I first came into the revelation of breaking curses as I began to minister deliverance to people in my local church. One particular case involved a young lady who came for prayer because of suicidal tendencies.

As I and other workers began to cast out numerous spirits, we encountered a strong demon that refused to leave. The more we would command it to go, the more it would keep saying, "No." After about twenty minutes of this, I commanded the spirit to tell me what legal right it had to stay. The spirit responded, "A curse."

This spirit stated that the young lady's parents had been involved in witchcraft. I then broke all curses of witchcraft from the young lady's life and commanded the evil spirit to leave. The spirit then came out screaming. From this, I began to understand how curses not only open the door for demons, but also give demons a legal right to remain and operate.

Therefore, understanding the nature of curses is a key to deliverance. When curses are broken and evil spirits are cast out, the person's life begins to dramatically change. This is God's answer to a curse—deliverance! There is only one solution—GOD'S! The problem (a curse) and the solution (deliverance) are found in the Word of God.

Chapter Five

The Solution

Ye have sown much, and bring in little; ye eat, but ye have not enough; ye drink, but ye are not filled with drink; ye clothe you, but there is none warm; and he that earneth wages earneth wages to put it into a bag with holes. Thus saith the LORD of hosts; Consider your ways.
—Haggai 1:6–7

Haggai 1:6 gives us a picture of what it feels like to be under a curse. It describes a condition. In verse 7, the prophet gives the reason why the people were in this condition. He gives the word of the Lord, which was, *"Consider your ways."* In other words, the people were in this condition because of their ways.

When our ways are contrary to the ways of God, we will end up in trouble. In order to come out from under the curse, we must change our ways. Often people living under a curse never take time to "consider their ways." *To consider* means "to think of, especially with regard to taking some action." It means "to reflect or deliberate." We cannot continue to live lives contrary to the Word of God and expect to escape curses.

After a person has considered his ways, he needs to repent. *To repent* means "to turn from your wicked ways." Without repentance, there is no deliverance. Breaking a curse, based on Galatians 3:13, along with a prayer of repentance, is necessary to come out from under the curse.

Repentance, Breaking the Curse, Deliverance

The first thing you as a believer need to know is that you are redeemed from the Curse (Galatians 3:13), and that no matter what sins have been committed or what doors have been opened in previous generations, there is forgiveness and deliverance in Christ.

When you repent, you turn around and turn away from sin. Repentance is the result of godly sorrow. *"Godly sorrow worketh repentance to salvation"* (2 Corinthians 7:10). Put another way, the result of godly sorrow is repentance, which leads to salvation, which means deliverance.

After repentance comes the actual breaking of the curse. This is done in the name of Jesus. We have authority to break curses based on Galatians 3:13.

Once curses are broken, the legal grounds used by demon spirits to remain in a person's life are taken

The Solution

away. The next step is commanding the spirits that have operated in that person's life to come out, in Jesus' name.

Breaking Curses

> *Christ hath redeemed us from the curse of the law, being made a curse for us: for it is written, Cursed is every one that hangeth on a tree.* *(Galatians 3:13)*

Again, curses are broken based on this verse of Scripture. This verse speaks of our redemption as legal, but not automatic. What Jesus purchased for us through His blood on the cross has to be appropriated by faith. If we have trusted in the atoning work of Christ, then as far as eternal salvation is concerned, we are secure.

However, as far as curses are concerned, believers can still be affected. Curses need to be identified and broken in the lives of believers. Breaking the curse takes away the legal right demons have to operate. After the legal grounds are destroyed, demons can be forced to manifest themselves and be cast out in the name of the Lord Jesus Christ!

Remember, curses are often generational. They can affect many generations after the iniquity has been committed. Some curses need to be broken five, ten, twenty, and even twenty-five generations back on both sides of the family.

Identifying and Breaking Curses

Prayer of Deliverance

Heavenly Father, I repent of any sins in my life or my ancestors' lives that have resulted in a curse. I repent of all disobedience, rebellion, perversion, witchcraft, idolatry, lust, adultery, fornication, mistreatment of others, murder, cheating, lying, sorcery, divination, and occult involvement. I ask for Your forgiveness and cleansing through the blood of the Lord Jesus Christ.

I take authority over and break any and every curse upon my life in the name of Jesus. I break all curses of poverty, lack, debt, destruction, sickness, death, and vagabondism. I break all curses on my marriage, family, children, and relationships. I break curses of rejection, pride, rebellion, lust, hurt, incest, rape, Ahab, Jezebel, fear, insanity, madness, and confusion.

I break all curses affecting my finances, mind, sexual character, emotions, will, and relationships.

I break every hex, jinx, spell, and spoken curse over my life.

I break every fetter, shackle, chain, cord, habit, and cycle that is the result of a curse.

According to Galatians 3:13, I have been redeemed from *"the curse of the law"* by the sacrifice of Jesus. I exercise my faith in the blood of Jesus and loose myself and my descendants from any and every curse. I claim forgiveness through the blood of Jesus for the sins of the fathers.

All of my sins have been remitted, and I loose myself from the curses that came as a result of all disobedience and rebellion to the Word of God.

I exercise my faith, and I know that confession is made unto salvation (Romans 10:10). Therefore, I confess that Abraham's blessings are mine (Galatians 3:14). I am not cursed, but blessed. I am *"the head, and not the tail"* (Deuteronomy 28:13). I am above and not beneath (verse 13). I am blessed coming in and blessed going out. I am blessed, and what God has blessed cannot be cursed.

I command spirits of rejection, hurt, bitterness, unforgiveness, bondage, torment, death, destruction, fear, lust, perversion, mind control, witchcraft, poverty, lack, debt, confusion, double-mindedness, sickness, infirmity, pain, divorce, separation, strife, contention, depression, sadness, loneliness, self-pity, self-destruction, self-rejection, anger, rage, wrath, anguish, vagabondism, abuse, and addiction to come out in the name of Jesus!

Identifying and Breaking Curses

Lord, I thank You for setting me free from every curse and every spirit that has operated in my life as the result of a curse. Amen.

*****

After praying this prayer of deliverance, it may be necessary to receive special prayer from experienced deliverance workers for deliverance. Remember, breaking curses removes the legal grounds that demons have to remain and operate in a person's life. Breaking the curse is often the first step to deliverance. The next step is the actual casting out of demons.

Scripture References regarding Curses

Cursed be the man that maketh any graven or molten image, an abomination unto the Lord, the work of the hands of the craftsman, and putteth it in a secret place. And all the people shall answer and say, Amen. Cursed be he that setteth light by his father or his mother. And all the people shall say, Amen. Cursed be he that removeth his neighbour's landmark. And all the people shall say, Amen. Cursed be he that maketh the blind to wander out of the way. And all the people shall say, Amen. Cursed be he that perverteth the judgment of the stranger, fatherless, and widow. And all the people shall say, Amen. Cursed be he that lieth with his father's wife; because he uncovereth his father's skirt. And all the people shall say, Amen. Cursed be he that lieth with any manner of beast. And all the people shall say, Amen. Cursed be he that

lieth with his sister, the daughter of his father, or the daughter of his mother. And all the people shall say, Amen. Cursed be he that lieth with his mother in law. And all the people shall say, Amen. Cursed be he that smiteth his neighbour secretly. And all the people shall say, Amen. Cursed be he that taketh reward to slay an innocent person. And all the people shall say, Amen. Cursed be he that confirmeth not all the words of this law to do them. And all the people shall say, Amen.
(Deuteronomy 27:15–26)

But it shall come to pass, if thou wilt not hearken unto the voice of the Lᴏʀᴅ thy God, to observe to do all his commandments and his statutes which I command thee this day; that all these curses shall come upon thee, and overtake thee: Cursed shalt thou be in the city, and cursed shalt thou be in the field. Cursed shall be thy basket and thy store. Cursed shall be the fruit of thy body, and the fruit of thy land, the increase of thy kine, and the flocks of thy sheep. Cursed shalt thou be when thou comest in, and cursed shalt thou be when thou goest out. The Lᴏʀᴅ shall send upon thee cursing, vexation, and rebuke, in all that thou settest thine hand unto for to do, until thou be destroyed, and until thou perish quickly; because of the wickedness of thy doings, whereby thou hast forsaken me. The Lᴏʀᴅ shall make the pestilence cleave unto thee, until he have consumed thee from off the land, whither thou goest to possess it. The Lᴏʀᴅ shall smite thee with a consumption, and with a fever, and with an inflammation, and with an extreme burning, and with the sword, and with blasting, and with mildew; and they shall pursue thee until thou perish. And thy heaven that is over thy head shall be brass, and the earth that is under thee shall be iron. The LORD shall make the rain of thy land powder and dust: from heaven shall it come down upon thee, until thou be destroyed. The LORD shall cause thee to be smitten before thine enemies: thou shalt go out one way against them, and flee seven ways before them: and shalt be removed into all the kingdoms of the earth. And thy carcase shall be meat unto all fowls of the air, and unto the beasts of the earth, and no man shall fray them away. The LORD will smite thee with the botch of Egypt, and with the emerods, and with the scab, and with the itch, whereof thou canst not be healed. The LORD shall smite thee with madness, and blindness, and aston-ishment of heart: and thou shalt grope at noonday, as the blind gropeth in darkness, and thou shalt not prosper in thy ways: and thou shalt be only oppressed and spoiled evermore, and no man shall save thee. Thou shalt betroth a wife, and another man shall lie with her: thou shalt build an house, and thou shalt not dwell therein: thou shalt plant a vineyard, and shalt not gather the grapes thereof. Thine ox shall be slain before thine eyes, and thou shalt not eat thereof: thine ass shall be violently taken away from before thy face, and shall not be restored to thee: thy sheep shall be given unto thine enemies, and thou shalt have none to rescue them. Thy sons and thy daughters shall be given unto another people, and thine eyes shall look, and fail with longing for them all the day long: and there shall be no might in thine hand. The fruit of thy land, and all thy labours, shall a nation which thou knowest not eat up; and thou shalt be only oppressed and crushed alway: so that thou shalt be mad for the sight of thine eyes which thou shalt see. The LORD *shall smite thee in the knees, and in the legs, with a sore botch that cannot be healed, from the sole of thy foot unto the top of thy head. The* LORD *shall bring thee, and thy king which thou shalt set over thee, unto a nation which neither thou nor thy fathers have known; and there shalt thou serve other gods, wood and stone. And thou shalt become an astonishment, a proverb, and a byword, among all nations whither the* LORD *shall lead thee. Thou shalt carry much seed out into the field, and shalt gather but little in; for the locust shall consume it. Thou shalt plant vineyards, and dress them, but shalt neither drink of the wine, nor gather the grapes; for the worms shall eat them. Thou shalt have olive trees throughout all thy coasts, but thou shalt not anoint thyself with the oil; for thine olive shall cast his fruit. Thou shalt beget sons and daughters, but thou shalt not enjoy them; for they shall go into captivity. All thy trees and fruit of thy land shall the locust consume. The stranger that is within thee shall get up above thee very high; and thou shalt come down very low. He shall lend to thee, and thou shalt not lend to him: he shall be the head, and thou shalt be the tail. Moreover all these curses shall come upon thee, and shall pursue thee, and overtake thee, till thou be destroyed; because thou hearkenedst not unto the voice of the* LORD *thy God, to keep his commandments and his statutes which he commanded thee: and they shall be upon thee for a sign and for a wonder, and upon thy seed for ever. Because thou servedst not the* LORD *thy God with joyfulness, and with gladness of heart, for the abundance of all things; therefore shalt thou serve thine enemies which the LORD shall send against thee, in hunger, and in thirst, and in nakedness, and in want of all things: and he shall put a yoke of iron upon thy neck, until he have destroyed thee. The LORD shall bring a nation against thee from far, from the end of the earth, as swift as the eagle flieth; a nation whose tongue thou shalt not understand; a nation of fierce countenance, which shall not regard the person of the old, nor show favour to the young: and he shall eat the fruit of thy cattle, and the fruit of thy land, until thou be destroyed: which also shall not leave thee either corn, wine, or oil, or the increase of thy kine, or flocks of thy sheep, until he have destroyed thee. And he shall besiege thee in all thy gates, until thy high and fenced walls come down, wherein thou trustedst, throughout all thy land: and he shall besiege thee in all thy gates throughout all thy land, which the LORD thy God hath given thee. And thou shalt eat the fruit of thine own body, the flesh of thy sons and of thy daughters, which the LORD thy God hath given thee, in the siege, and in the straitness, wherewith thine enemies shall distress thee: so that the man that is tender among you, and very delicate, his eye shall be evil toward his brother, and toward the wife of his bosom, and toward the remnant of his children which he shall leave: so that he will not give to any of them of the flesh of his children whom he shall eat: because he hath nothing left him in the siege, and in the straitness, wherewith thine enemies shall distress thee in all thy gates. The tender and delicate woman among you, which would not adventure to set the sole of her foot upon the ground for delicateness and tenderness, her eye shall be evil toward the husband of her bosom, and toward her son, and toward her daughter, and toward her young one that cometh out from between her feet, and toward her children which she shall bear: for she shall eat them for want of all things secretly in the siege and straitness, wherewith thine enemy shall distress thee in thy gates. If thou wilt not observe to do all the words of this law that are written in this book, that thou mayest fear this glorious and fearful name, THE LORD THY GOD; then the LORD will make thy plagues wonderful, and the plagues of thy seed, even great plagues, and of long continuance, and sore sicknesses, and of long continuance. Moreover he will bring upon thee all the diseases of Egypt, which thou wast afraid of; and they shall cleave unto thee. Also every sickness, and every plague, which is not written in the book of this law, them will the LORD bring upon thee, until thou be destroyed. And ye shall be left few in number, whereas ye were as the stars of heaven for multitude; because thou wouldest not obey the voice of the LORD thy God. And it shall come to pass, that as the LORD rejoiced over you to do you good, and to multiply you; so the LORD will rejoice over you to destroy you, and to bring you to nought; and ye shall be plucked from off the land whither thou goest to possess it. And the LORD shall scatter thee among all people, from the one end of the earth even unto the other; and there thou shalt serve other gods, which neither thou nor thy fathers have known, even wood and stone. And among these nations shalt thou find no ease, neither shall the sole of thy foot have rest: but the LORD shall give thee there a trembling heart, and failing of eyes, and sorrow of mind: and thy life shall hang in doubt before thee; and thou shalt fear day and night, and shalt have none assurance of thy life: in the morning thou shalt say, Would God it were even! and at even thou shalt say, Would God it were morning! for the fear of thine heart wherewith thou shalt fear, and for the sight of thine eyes which thou shalt see. And the LORD shall bring thee into Egypt again with ships, by the way whereof I spake unto thee, Thou shalt see it no more again: and there ye shall be sold unto your enemies for bondmen and bondwomen, and no man shall buy you.* (Deuteronomy 28:15–68)

Appendix

Tactics to Rout Demons
(from *Annihilating the Hosts of Hell*, by Win Worley)

A Way for the Deliverance Worker to Get Started

1. Brief conversations about the reason the person is there for ministry.

2. General prayer and worship—focus on God and His goodness, power, and so on.

3. Bind the powers over the area. Break assignments—from powers in the air to demons in the person. Ask for angelic protection (Hebrews 1:14).

4. Ask and receive by faith the gifts of the Spirit needed to minister.

Leadership during Deliverance Time

1. Too many people commanding spirits (different ones) at the same time causes confusion for

everyone, especially for the person being ministered to.

2. Leadership will often shift as the Holy Spirit directs.

3. Husbands are often the most effective in commanding spirits to leave their wives, with the support of others.

Tactics for Speaking to Demons

1. Address the spirit by name, and if that is not known, address by function.

    a. Either the Holy Spirit will give it, or the demon will reveal himself.
    b. Do not rely on either method *exclusively*—be open to the Holy Spirit in this area.

2. Repeatedly remind these spirits that your authority is given to you by Jesus Christ, who is far above all rule and authority (Ephesians 1:20–21).

3. Remind them of their fate in Revelation 20:10 and other places in Scripture (Job 30:3–8). Use the statement, "The Lord Jesus Christ rebukes you," repeatedly, as a battering ram. (See Jude 9.)

4. It is helpful to harass the demons to confess that Jesus Christ is their Lord.

5. Ruler demons often can be badgered for more information.

6. At times you will command the ruler demon to go, and then clean out the lesser demons under him, and if that does not work, reverse the tactic.

7. Bind and separate interfering spirits as God leads.

8. There is no need to shout at demons since the battle is not in the flesh, but in the Spirit.

What to Expect in Receiving Deliverance

While many deliverances involve obvious physical manifestations, not all demons react in this manner. Some spirits leave quietly and nonviolently.

You may not have a strong physical reaction when receiving deliverance; therefore, don't be disappointed if you don't receive deliverance in this manner. What you should expect is a release. You know there is a release when...

1. Oppressive force disappears

2. Heaviness lifts

3. Uneasiness goes away

4. Burden or load lightens

5. There is an inner sense of liberty, freedom, and divine satisfaction or contentment

6. The joy of the Lord comes, and you are able to rejoice!

Identifying and Breaking Curses

The result of deliverance is righteousness, peace, and joy in the Holy Spirit (Romans 14:17). When devils are cast out, the kingdom of God has come (Matthew 12:28).

Demon Manifestations

When evil spirits depart, you can normally expect some sort of manifestation through the mouth or nose of a person.

Listed below are some of the common manifestations:

1. Coughing

2. Drooling

3. Vomiting

4. Spitting

5. Foaming

6. Crying

7. Screaming

8. Sighing

9. Roaring

10. Belching

11. Yawning

12. Exhaling

Appendix

Again, when demons are cast out, they normally leave through the mouth or the nose. Spirits are associated with breathing. Both the Hebrews and the Greeks had only one word for spirit and breath. In the Greek, that word is *pneuma*. The Holy Spirit is breathed in (John 20:22). Evil spirits are breathed out.

Sometimes people shake or tremble when they receive deliverance. Their bodies, in whole or part, may actually shake or tremble.

Hindrances to Receiving Deliverance

1. Curses

2. Sin

3. Pride

4. Passivity

5. Ungodly soul ties

6. Occultism

7. Fear

8. Embarrassment

9. Unbelief

10. Lack of desire

11. Unforgiveness

12. Lack of knowledge

Identifying and Breaking Curses

All demons have legal, biblical grounds when they oppress people. They may not torment at will. If demons have legal grounds, then they have the right to remain. These legal grounds must be destroyed in order to receive and maintain deliverance.

How to Keep Your Deliverance

1. Read God's Word daily.

2. Find a group of Bible-believing people, preferably a church, and regularly meet with them for worship, study, and ministry.

3. Pray with the understanding and in tongues (1 Corinthians 14:15).

4. Place the blood of Jesus on yourself and your family.

5. Determine as nearly as you can which spirits have been cast out of you. Make a list, for these areas Satan will try to recapture.

6. The way demons gain reentry is through a lax, undisciplined thought life. The mind is the battlefield. You must cast down imaginations, and bring every thought into the obedience of Christ (2 Corinthians 10:5).

7. Pray to the Father fervently, asking Him to make you alert, sober, and vigilant against wrong thoughts (1 Peter 5:8–9).

Appendix

8. The demons signal their approach to you by the fact that the old thought patterns you once had are now trying to return unto you. As soon as this happens, immediately rebuke them. State *verbally* that you refuse them, as quickly as possible.

9. You have the authority to loose the *angels of the Lord* to battle the demons (Hebrews 1:14; Matthew 18:18). Bind the demons and loose upon them the spirits of destruction (1 Chronicles 21:12) and burning and judgment (Isaiah 4:4) from the Lord Jesus Christ. Also, loose warrior angels upon the demons.

About the Author

John Eckhardt is called to impart and activate the gifts of the Spirit in order to raise up strong ministries in the body of Christ. A gifted man with a true apostolic and prophetic call on his life, his desire is to infiltrate the world with the Word of God. He is dedicated to perfecting the saints and training ministers to fulfill the call of God on their lives. Along with his apostolic and pastoral responsibilities, John Eckhardt produces a daily radio broadcast and "Perfecting the Saints," a daily television program, and he ministers throughout the United States and overseas.

John Eckhardt resides in a suburb of Chicago with his lovely wife, Wanda, and their five children.

To order books and tapes by John Eckhardt,
please write or call:

Crusaders I.M.P.A.C.T.
P.O. Box 492
Matteson, IL 60422
(708) 922-0983